Neg[ative]

Thoughts

How to Rewire the
Thought Process and
Flush out Negative
Thinking, Depression,
and Anxiety Without
Resorting to Harmful
Meds

This document is geared towards providing exact and reliable information in regards to the topic and issue covered. The publication is sold with the idea that the publisher is not required to render accounting, officially permitted, or otherwise, qualified services. If advice is necessary, legal or professional, a practiced individual in the profession should be ordered.

- From a Declaration of Principles which was accepted and approved equally by a Committee of the American Bar Association and a Committee of Publishers and Associations.

prohibited and any storage of this document is not allowed unless with written permission from the publisher. All rights reserved.

The information provided herein is stated to be truthful and consistent, in that any liability, in terms of inattention or otherwise, by any usage or abuse of any policies, processes, or directions contained within is the solitary and utter responsibility of the recipient reader. Under no circumstances will any legal responsibility or blame be held against the publisher for any reparation, damages, or monetary loss due to the information herein, either directly or indirectly.

Respective authors own all copyrights not held by the publisher.

The information herein is offered for informational purposes solely, and is universal as so. The presentation of the information is

Contents

Introduction

Research demonstrates that over 90% of the things that people with mood disorders such as depression are actually negative and self-destructive. This negative self-discussion eventually prospects to a self-fulfilling prophecy - what we're constantly repeating in our brains eventually creates a damaging mindset that ends up making our recurrent self-talk a reality. Negative thoughts boost your levels of unhappiness and can ultimately damage your quality of life. It can eventually lead you to an unhealthy and self-destructive path. Luckily, on the other hand, positive self-chat can have the opposite effect - it can help you become a healthier, happier, well informed, and more competent person.

Optimists are usually good at detecting any negative self-talk patterns and disabling them or replacing them with more positive thoughts, so that they don't end up impacting their lives the wrong way. Although you might have believed that people are born being optimists, it is actually quite possible to train your thought process and transform it into one with a more positive outlook with some practice and self-awareness.

Realistic, practical optimism is a choice you may make on purpose to help manage your daily life. There exists a group of characteristics that a lot of optimists have as a common factor, but through smart use of certain strategies normally utilized by hem, even hardcore pessimists can eventually change the way their minds work.

What realistic, practical optimism isn't:

- Denying reality
- Putting a band aid over problems
- Pointless hoping
- Self-deluded thinking
- Purposely Ignorant thinking

What it actually is:

- An effective management method for confronting problems

- A way to select the best outcomes from life.

- A method for dealing with life's challenges.

- A long-term happier, healthier lifestyle.

Every one of us has lived through a unique collection of encounters that has deeply impacted the way of seeing our world. This includes our interests, needs and wants, values, and psychological tendencies. We all have been born with coping capabilities which constantly shift every day. As we develop, our coping mechanisms may become weaker or more powerful, which eventually affects the positive or negative way we view the world.

It was previously believed in medical literature, specifically psychiatry, that people react to life's stresses in several ways which include avoidance and repression. Now we all know that everyone is born with the ability to manage stress, however, some can have a harder time developing naturally the required skills to do so effectively.

One of the great things about being sentient human being is that we always have a choice of changing our behaviors and patterns. We have the ability to realize what is making us manage challenging situations in our world and also the things that are constantly impeding that. We are able to check our views on life and completely replace less efficient methods for coping.

Chapter 1: Taking proper care of your mental health

Techniques to calm the mind and replace negative thoughts with positive ones can be incredibly beneficial for our mental health. However, one of the smartest things to do before using those techniques is to focus on taking care or your mental health in a similar fashion that someone would build up their physical well-being.

Your mental health influences the way you think, feel, and behave in your day to day life. Additionally, it affects your stress management potential and ability to overcome challenges, engage with others, and get over life's setbacks and hardships. Whether you're searching to handle a particular mental health condition, manage your feelings in a more convenient and efficient manner, or just feel better and more energetic, there are many steps you can take to dramatically kick-start your journey towards a more optimistic view of life without depending on medication.

The connection between resilience and mental health

Being psychologically healthy does not mean never dealing with bad occasions or experiencing emotional issues. All of us undergo disappointments, loss, and drastic changes in our lives. Even though all of these are normal parts of our existence, they are still able to cause a great deal of sadness, depression, and stress. As you are probably already aware, physically fit individuals are able to better recover from illness or injuries. The same rings true for individuals with strong mental health, as they are able to better recover from adversity, trauma, and stress. This ability is known as resilience.

Those who are emotionally and psychologically resilient possess the tools to help cope with difficult situations and maintain a positive frame-of-mind after being faced with hardship. They continue to be focused, flexible, and efficient in bad occasions - in both good and tough times. Their resilience also means they are less scared of something totally new or perhaps an uncertain future event. Even when they won't immediately understand how an issue can get resolved, they won't have much trouble keeping their calm and being aware that they will be able to eventually find a solution.

Using your mental health (yes, it is possible!)

Anybody can be afflicted by mental or emotional health issues - over the course of their lifetimes, the vast majority of people will. There's no way around this fact. In the winter season alone, about 1 in 5 people are affected from some kind of mental disorder. Yet, despite how common mental health issues are, a lot of us don't give them enough importance and never take action to try to improve the situation.

We disregard the emotional messages from our body informing us something is wrong and try to distract ourselves or self-medicate with alcohol, drugs, or self-destructive behaviours. We disregard important matters affecting our lives and hope that others will not notice. We hope that things will ultimately improve by themselves. Or we just admit defeat-telling ourselves this really is just the way we are and there's no way around it.

The good thing is: it's not necessary to embrace this self-defeat. There's many steps you can take to help you raise your mood, be more resilient, and improve your quality of life exponentially. Just as it takes some effort to build up physical health, there's some work involved in developing a healthy mind. We must continually work towards the goal of a healthier mind, since there are several things that can take a toll on our emotional state these days.

How come we are frequently unable to deal with our mental health needs?

Our lack of ability to deal with our mental health needs stems from a number of reasons:

In certain societies, emotional and mental issues are noticed as less important or 'legitimate' than physical issues. They are even seen as a manifestation of weakness or in some way to be our very own fault.

Many people mistakenly see mental health issues as something we ought to know how to deactivate or 'snap out of' without little to no effort. Men especially, are frequently known for keeping their feelings and emotional issues to themselves and never seek help, as they feel it may go against their masculinity.

Nowadays, we're obsessed by seeking simple solutions to complex problems. Some have replaced the feeling of connection you get by being with others by simply checking social media, which is quicker and available at all times. Instead of putting in some effort to improve our mood, when we are looking to ease depression or anxiety we take a pill, which in several cases acts only as a band aid to the actual problem.

Lots of people believe that when they do seek help for emotional and mental problems, the only real treatments they have as an option are: medication (which usually comes with undesirable negative effects) or therapy (which may be extended and costly). The fact is that, whatever your issue is, you will find steps you can take to enhance how you feel and experience greater emotional and mental well-being. And you can even start doing them today!

Make social connection important-especially face-to-face

Regardless of how much time you spend by yourself improving your emotional and mental state, you still need to be around others to feel and function at your best. There's no way around this. Humans are social creatures with emotional needs for relationships and positive connections to other people. We're not designed to survive, not to mention thrive, in isolation. Our social brains crave companionship-even if experience makes us shy and distrustful of others.

Why are real interactions with others so essential?

Audio or video calls and social media can be useful, but they won't provide you with the same stress eliminating and mental health-boosting power that real interactions with other people will give you.

The most important thing is to interact with somebody that is a great listener-someone you are able to regularly speak won't have any preconceive ideas of how you should think or behave or judge you negatively. A great listener will pay attention to the emotions behind what you are saying, and will not interrupt, judge, or criticize you.

Reaching out to others should not be considered as a sign of weak character and when done considerately, you will never be an encumbrance to others. In fact, most people will be very flattered if they find that you have enough confidence in them for you to open up to them. If you do not feel you have anybody to go to at the moment, there's still lots of benefit you can get from interacting face-to-face with acquaintances or people you encounter throughout the day, for example neighbours, individuals at the checkout line or around the bus, or even the person serving you your morning coffee. Don't be afraid to smile at them, make some eye contact and engage in small talk.

Strategies for connecting to other people

Call a buddy or family member now and decide to get together. Should you both lead busy lives, offer to help with errands or do a healthy activity, such as exercising together. Try to frame it as a normal get-together.

Reaching out to acquaintances. If you aren't able to find someone in your family or social circle to spend time with, try reaching out to old friends. Not everyone finds it easy to make new friends, so you can try going with a co-worker out for supper, or asking a neighbour to have coffee with you.

Escape from your TV or computer monitor.
Communication is really a largely non-verbal
experience that requires you to stay in direct
contact with others, so don't neglect your real-world
relationships by favouring spending time in front of
the TV or Computer.

Join new groups. If you do some search, you'll
probably find that there's several groups with
people with common interests. This is probably one
of the easiest and quickest ways to make new
friends or connect with others. Small talk won't be
hard at all!

**Never be afraid to smile and greet other
people you cross paths in your day to day
life.** Creating a connection is advantageous to
everyone involved-and who knows where it might
lead!

The importance of staying active

Your mental health influences the way you think, feel, and behave in daily existence. Additionally, it affects what you can do to handle stress, overcome challenges, engage, and get over life's setbacks and hardships. Whether you're searching to handle a particular mental health condition, handle your feelings better, or just to feel better and more energetic, there are many steps you can take to balance your mental health-beginning today.

What if you hate exercising?

Well, you aren't alone. Pounding weights inside a gym or jogging on the treadmill isn't everyone's cup of tea, but it's not necessary to be considered a fitness fanatic to get the benefits of being a more physically active person. Even light physical activities such as going for a walk at lunchtime, walking laps at an air-conditioned mall while shopping for stuff, playing Frisbee with your dog, dancing to songs, playing activity-based game titles together with your kids or cycling for an appointment instead of driving – all work.

It's not necessary to work out until you're drenched in sweat or every muscle aches. Even modest levels of exercise can produce a huge difference for your emotional and mental health-and it is something can do today to increase your energy and positive outlook on life, which helps you get back a feeling of control.

Strategies for starting a physical exercise routine

Strive for at least half an hour of physical activity 3 to 5 days per week. 3 short sessions of 10 minutes split throughout the day also works. You can even begin today by walking or dancing to your favourite music.

Try rhythmic exercise that engages your legs and arms, for example walking, running, swimming, weight lifting, practicing a martial art, or dancing.

Add an extra layer of mindfulness to your physical activity routine. Rather of being focused on your ideas and thoughts when exercising, try concentrating on the way your body feels while you're in motion – for example, focus on how your breathing changes or the temperature of the wind touching your skin.

Learn to keep your stress threshold under control

Stress eventually puts a very heavy toll on your emotional and mental well-being, so it's vital to be keeping it in check constantly. Whilst not all stress factors can be prevented, stress management strategies can help tremendously. Here's a few ideas:

Speak with someone friendly. Face-to-face social interaction with somebody that cares for you and likes you for who you are is one of the best way to calm your central nervous system as well as to reduce stress. Interacting with someone else can quickly limit damaging stress reactions from your body such as the 'fight or flight' response. Additionally, it will help your body produce stress- eliminating hormones naturally, so you'll feel good even when you are not able to change the challenging situation itself.

Indulge a bit. Does hearing an uplifting song cause you to feel more relaxed? Or perhaps you feel better when you're smelling ground coffee or another scent you're fond of? Or maybe it's something as simple as squeezing a stress ball that makes you feel calmer. Everybody reacts to sensory stimulus just a little differently, so start experimenting and learn to determine what works well for you. When you learn which ways your central nervous system reacts to sensory input, you'll be able to quickly resort to 'hacks' that will help you feel better immediately.

The importance of leisure time. Do stuff without other reason than they feel extremely nice to do them. Watch a comedy, go to the beach, listen to your favourite music, read a great book, or speak with a buddy. Doing things just because they are fun is not a bad thing. Leisure time is definitely a mental and emotional health necessity.

Contemplation and appreciation in your life. Consider the items you're grateful for. Meditate, pray (if you're religiously inclined), watch the sunset, or just take the time to concentrate on what's good, positive, and delightful along the way regarding your day.

Consciously practicing relaxation. While physical input can relieve stress within the moment, relaxation techniques will help lower your overall stress levels -

although they're prone to be hard in the beginning before you start reaping the rewards. Yoga, mindfulness meditation, breathing, or progressive muscle relaxation can put stress to a halt and take your body and mind back to a healthier and more balanced state.

How a brain-healthy diet can help you have solid mental health

Unless of course you've attempted to modify your diet previously, you might not be familiar with how much our food choices affect how you think and feel. A poor diet will eventually take a toll in your brain and mood, disrupt your sleep, decrease your energy, and weaken your body's immune system efficiency. On the other hand, switching to a healthy diet, one that's lower in sugar and wealthy in healthy fats, can provide you with more energy, enhance your sleep and mood, and enable you to feel and look your very best.

People will have varied responses to different foods, mostly based on genetics along with other health factors, so experiment a little to better understand the way the food you use in-or cut from-your diet plan changes how you feel. A good place to start can be something simple, such as to eliminate the "bad fats" from your diet or sweets. Any fats that may damage your mood and outlook, you and simply replace with "good fats" that support brain-health. The same goes with sugar – opt for complex carb foods instead.

Foods that adversely affect mood

-Caffeine

-Alcohol

-Trans fats or anything that includes "partly hydrogenated" oil

-Foods rich in amounts of preservative chemicals or hormones

-Sugary snacks

-Refined carbs (for example white-colored grain or white-colored flour)

-Fried food

Foods that boost mood

-Fatty fish wealthy in Omega-3s for example salmon, sardines, spanish mackerel, anchovies, sardines, tuna

-Nuts. For example walnuts, almonds, cashews, peanuts

-Avocados

-Flaxseed

-Beans

-Leafy vegetables for example green spinach, kale, the city sprouts

-Fruit, especially if low in sugar and high on nutrients and antioxidants. Berries are an excellent choice.

The importance of sleep

If you're currently leading an active and busy life, reducing sleep may seem to be a smart idea on the surface. But regarding your mental (and physical) health, getting enough sleep is an absolute necessity. The idea of sleep being a luxury is very antiquated. Skipping a few hours per week can quickly take a toll in your mood, energy, mental sharpness, and stress management capabilities. And also over time, chronic sleep loss can completely ruin your wellbeing and outlook.

While adults should strive for seven to nine hrs of quality sleep every night, it can be difficult to get more than 5 or 6 if you simply close your eyes and hope for the best. Your mind needs time for you to unwind when you go to bed. One of the first things you should do is staying away from bright screen-TVs, phones, tablets, computers-within the 1-2 hrs before bed time. Also important is putting away work, and postponing arguments, worrying, or brainstorming until the following day.

Strategies for improving sleep

If anxiety or chronic worrying dominates your ideas during the night, you will find that there's several things you can do to learn to relax a bit.

To relax, calm your brain, and get ready for sleep, try the following: taking a warm shower, reading a relaxing book with a soft light, hearing soothing music, or practicing your favourite relaxation technique.

To assist set your body's internal clock and optimize your sleeping patterns, try to stay with a normal sleep-wake schedule, even on weekends.

Make certain your bed room is dark, a bit on the cold side, and quiet. Curtains, white-noise devices and fans might help to distract your mind.

Find purpose and meaning in existence

Everybody derives meaning and purpose in their own unique ways, and they may involve doing stuff that benefit others, in addition to yourself. Having a mission or an important goal in life can be used as a method to make yourself feel needed in the world. It will also help yourself to get up every morning. Believe it or not, in biological terms, finding meaning and purpose is important to brain health as it can certainly help generate new cells and promote optimal function. It may also boost your immune system, alleviate discomfort, relieve stress, and inspire you to pursue other more demanding steps to find better emotional and mental health. However, you derive meaning and purpose in existence, it's vital that you try to do those things every single day.

Why is finding purpose in your life important? Doing stuff that challenges your creativeness will make you feel productive, which in turn can greatly support your mental health. This will be explored further in another chapter. It doesn't matter whether you receive money for such things or not. Things such as gardening, drawing, writing, playing a musical instrument, or building something inside your workshop are all great ways of developing your creative side.

Relationships. Spending time in which you help individuals that matter to you, whether they are buddies, grandkids, or seniors relatives, supports not only their well-being, but yours too. It will also supply you with a great feeling purpose in your life.

Taking care of a dog or a cat. Yes, pets can be a significant responsibility, but taking care of another being can do wonders for making you feel needed and loved. It's no secret why pets are recommended to people with mental disorders such as depression or PTSD. There is no love such as the unconditional love a pet can provide. Having pets may also help you get away and get some exercise or help you familiarize yourself with new people and places.

Volunteering. Just like we are hard-wired to be social creatures, we are also hard-wired to offer help to others. It has been proven time and again that your body produces high levels of feel good hormones whenever you do acts of kindness. There is no limit towards the individual and group volunteer possibilities you are able to explore. Schools, places of worship, non-profit organizations, and charitable organizations of all kinds rely on volunteers to stay afloat.

Caregiving. Taking proper care of an aging relative, a handicapped partner, or perhaps a child having a physical or mental illness are all acts of kindness. Love and loyalty could also be as rewarding and significant because it is challenging.

Chapter 2: The Powerful Effects of Positive and Negative Thinking

Our outlook and attitude on existence generally plays an enormous part in how happy we're in our day to day lives and just how effective we become. Somebody that thinks positively about everything can be more relaxed, calm and less stressed than somebody that often has a pessimistic mindset.

Not only does your thoughts affect your life, but additionally it also affects individuals surrounding you - in a nutshell, our mood affects everyone that we cross paths with. Developing and keeping a positive frame-of-mind is important if you want to guide an optimistic and fulfilling existence.

There are lots of ways that you are able to create a better outlook and start to alter the way you think and experience many situations that you simply encounter in day-to-day living. Altering your attitude and never sliding back to negative thinking will require time but eventually this brand new outlook will end up being an organic, natural part of your life. The 5 primary tips to keep in mind when altering your outlook on life through our thought process are:

1. Turn your thought process into positive thinking by exercising your thinking patterns every day. You need to set the mind on finishing one task at any given time and think only of the positive

outcome and just how good you'll feel if you have completed the job. Never surrender to doubt and allow yourself to believe you have done enough effort and quit.

2. Don't enable your conversations to turn negative. While in a discussion you can easily let others discourage you, particularly if they are individuals that have a pessimistic attitude towards life. Never be enticed to fall back to your old ways, and try to turn negative talk into a positive one in every event and situation.

3. Search for the positive in individuals surrounding you and let them know about it. This is an efficient way for you

to encourage an optimistic attitude everywhere.

4. Whatever you do inside your day-to-day existence look for something good inside it. Even if you're doing a dull task that you simply usually hate doing and something which leaves you feeling negatively, try to focus on something of it that will have a positive impact on you or others, no matter how small it may be.

5. Never allow yourself to become distracted or hoodwinked into returning to negativity. It requires time to adjust how you feel and think and if you've been lower on yourself and also the world for any lengthy amount of time, your new outlook will definitively take

some time to remain around enough to cause any significant impact.

6. You'll find with time that several aspects of your everyday life can be altered simply by modifying your outlook by shifting away from negativity onto something more positive. You will also notice that one's self-esteem improves since you are feeling happier and energized and you'll be able to tackle the duties you once hated without them causing unnecessary anxiety and stress. Expect your relationships to improve as well. These are merely some of the areas where one can self-improve and therefore lead a far more positive existence.

Being aware of your self-worth

Realizing one's self-worth is not at all related to checking the balance in your bank, but it's actually about you as an individual and where you fit in life. We give others respect, love and consideration but exactly how frequently will we give ourselves what's due? The way you value yourself is dependent on the self-esteem you've got, as one's self-esteem directly mirrors how much you care for yourself. Healthy self-esteem results in independence, happiness, versatility, the opportunity to adapt easily to unexpected circumstances, co- operation and a positive frame-of-mind on any situation. Unhealthy or low self- esteem however, leads often to irrational ideas, unhappiness, anxiety about unexpected situations, rigidity and defensiveness along with a negative outlook on existence.

The way we see ourselves offers quite a bit related to how others see us; if we are cheerful, smiling and filled with confidence, then others will see us as someone they would like to interact with. When we respect ourselves and portray this then you'll find that others will respect you back too. You've heard it before and it is true: how will you request respect from others if you're not able to respect yourself in the first place? Working on your self-worth is closely related to boosting your self-esteem, so let's take a more in-depth look at it.

High self-esteem

Here are a few of the most important traits found on people with high levels of self-esteem:

• They feel secure about who they are and trust their abilities

• They have no problem ultimately showing their true feelings to other people

• In relationships, their partners rarely complain about intimacy issues

• They are able to recognize and be proud of themselves for their achievements throughout life.

• They are easily in a position to forgive themselves for mistakes as well as forgive others.

Low self-esteem

On the other hand, let's take a look at some of the typical low self-esteem traits. If you're currently suffering from low self-esteem, you will probably recognize several of them:

• They do not believe in themselves and therefore are very insecure in several areas of their lives.

• They have problems showing and accepting closeness in relationships.

• They won't ever enable your true feelings show.

• They won't ever recognize and give themselves credit for their accomplishments.

• They have a hard time forgiving themselves or others.

• They resist change whenever possible.

Working on your self-worth

There are many ways that you are able to improve your self-esteem and shift towards a more positive and healthy outlook about yourself. Below are a few tips for gradually developing and increasing your self-worth.

• Don't take other's critique to heart. Instead, try paying attention to what they're saying and try to improve from it if the criticism is valid.

• Try to have a moment for yourself everyday where you are alone for a minutes, meditate, look inside yourself and realize all of your good attributes and picture altering your bad ones into something better.

• Celebrate and pride yourself on even the tiniest achievements that you are able to accomplish.

• Make an everyday activity that you simply enjoy, for example taking a stroll on a sunny day or soaking inside a warm bubble bath.

• Never deny yourself of something you enjoy if it will have a positive impact on your life, no matter how small it may be.

• Talk positively to yourself, repeat affirmations to thrust back all the negative ideas and feelings.

The advantages of using positive self-talk

Among the most useful tools that people may use to their benefit in life is actually found inside them. Particularly, we should be focusing on molding our thoughts and ideas due to the way they directly influence our feelings, and for that reason, they will have a profound impact on the way we cope with existence. By understanding how to control our self-talk and converting it into positive self-talk instead of negative (which many people do subconsciously during the day), you can start to achieve additional control over almost every facet of your day to day life by making essential changes.

Your ability to prosper largely depends upon the way you cope with existence; an optimistic mental attitude results in a confident and eventually more effective person, whereas an attitude filled with negativity results in too little self-confidence. Quality of life is largely dependent on the way you think and feel from moment to moment and altering how you think will be valuable in all stages of your life.

Someone who experiences existence optimistically by having a positive attitude is able to better cope with existence and the challenging circumstances it sometimes throws at us; they are also able to recover and get over problems or set-backs in less time. Someone with an optimistic attitude is able to view problems like what they truly are - only brief set-backs that they can overcome and move ahead. When viewing life within this frame of positivity, you will have the capacity to take full control of your ideas and feelings and make an adverse situation shift right into a better one simply by altering your thoughts. Since ideas may either be negative or positive and you are only able to have one thought in your mind at a certain time, then going for the positive could keep your thoughts, feelings and actions optimistic, which results in a happier person that can achieve the goals they've set with less effort and frustration.

Using positive self-talk inside your daily existence

You need to use positive self-talk during the day to be able to set up a new thinking pattern, as you've probably established a solid structure for negative thinking over several years. Realize that this will take some dedication to overcome. To begin with you need to try to engage in positive self-talk around 30-50 times during the day, which is accomplished by repeating positive statements silently to yourself or out aloud. If this sounds like a daunting task, realize that once you start feeling the effects of it, you'll probably become addicted in a good sense and you'll realize that there's little to no effort involved. Positive self-talk can be used in a variety of different ways in everyday life, as it can assist you to overcome difficult situations, gains in self-confidence, enable you to quit habits, recover faster from illness or make positive changes in your everyday life. Useful phrases you can use in positive self-talk include:

• I've got a fascinating challenge facing me - this may be used whenever a problem happens in existence or there's some difficulty. Instead of immediately triggering looking at the situation in a negative manner, and view it as a fascinating/interesting event, you'll find it much easier to cope with and actually accomplish something.

• I love the individual I am - this may be used to boost self-esteem and gain respect with regards to you and the person you are. Similar statements might be "I believe that I'm a good person", "I am a great person" or "I have numerous excellent qualities to offer to the world".

• I'm capable of doing this - this may be used if you're confronted with a particular task that you'd formerly doubt yourself to be able to conquer. Similarly you can say "I'm fully capable of conquering this" or "This doesn't pose a threat for me"

• I'm filled with health, energy and vitality - this can be used to inspire good feelings regarding your health either once you have been sick or while dealing with a disease.

• I'm feel fulfilled with myself as a person - this can be to inspire good general positive ideas with regards to you and the environment you're living in.

How affirmations can alter your existence

Getting an optimistic attitude is paramount to being happy and leading a fulfilling existence, our ideas play a crucial role in the way we feel, and positive thinking results in a confident person that's happy in their everyday life, while negativity results in low self-esteem and also on you passing up on a lot in existence. We so frequently talk ourselves from things without realizing we're doing them. Every day, countless negative ideas drift freely through our mind, and we put ourselves down time after time. There's a little simple tool which you can use during the day to assist in altering these negative ideas and instil a far more positive thought process. They will boost your confidence, awareness, and alter your existence in lots of different aspects for the better.

Defining positive affirmations.

Affirmations may be used during the day anywhere and whenever you feel like you need them. The more you use them, the easier it will be for positive ideas to take over negative ones and you'll be able to reap the rewards quicker. An affirmation is a straightforward technique which is used to alter the negative self-talk that we're rarely even conscious of doing. They can also help look at your with a more optimistic point of view. As mentioned previously, most people have bombarded themselves with negative thoughts for years, so altering their ideas and thought processes won't happen overnight. However, if you simply stick to doing these affirmations, they will become more and more effective the more you practice them. There are various affirmation techniques for coping with different situations in existence and typically the most popular and effective are highlighted below.

The mirror technique

This method allows you to appreciate yourself and develop self-awareness and self-esteem. You need to stand in front of a mirror, preferably a complete length one and be either naked or in your underwear. Start from top to bottom, starting with your head and saying aloud what it is that you like, appreciate, or find unique about the different areas of your body, for instance you can say: "I enjoy the way my hair shines, and its slight variations in color where the light hits it" or "My eyes really are a lovely shade of ___ _ _. They sparkle and glint. My eyes really are a wonderful feature" take some time and go gradually total the body accumulating a far more positive picture of yourself.

The anywhere technique

This method may be used anywhere and if you catch yourself thinking a negative thought. Whenever you find yourself in this situation, picture yourself as if you had a control knob within your mind that you can turn down low enough to the point where you can't hear it any longer. Then think about positive sentences to replace the negative ones and turn the volume back up while repeating these sentences in your mind.

The trashcan technique

For those who have negative ideas write them on the scrap of paper, screw the paper up right into a ball and throw it into a trashcan. This method actually works for lots of people that are struggling with negative thoughts. By using the trashcan technique you're telling yourself that these ideas aren't anything but rubbish and that the trash is where they belong.

The meditation technique

Find somewhere quiet in which you are able to relax for five or ten minutes. Close your eyes and allow your mid empty of ideas and feelings. Start to repeat positive affirmations about yourself again and again. While you're doing this, focus on the words you are repeating and say them with confidence.

Chapter 3: Is it all in your mind?

All of us undergo some tough events in our lives and there's no way around this fact. There's no reason why to make our minds our enemies throughout the tough times, so it will be extremely useful to know how to make it work with you and not against you.

However the most important question is "how can we maintain a positive attitude when things get tough?" Remaining upbeat in difficult situations is probably one of the last things on your mind, but it ought to be the very first, as it is crucially important to remain positive more than ever before. Here are a few useful strategies for keeping a positive frame-of-mind whenever you find yourself going through a rough patch:

• When you are around individuals who're negative try to keep away from them, as negativity has a means of being easily transferred from person to person.

• Don't sit while doing passive activities such as watching TV or viewing online videos for several hours at any given time. Programs such as news can easily increase feelings of depression or anxiety. Should you choose to watch TV or browse the internet, try choosing positive shows such as nature documentaries or non-negative comedy.

• Spend just as much time as possible with the family and family members, do activities together that you all enjoy and aim to have a family night at least one time per week where you can all spend time together

• In occasions when you're feeling particularly low and negativity begins to creep in, view a motivational video or repeat positive affirmations to yourself to recover an optimistic attitude.

• Take some time out every day to simply do something you enjoy doing that does not need you to make choices or decisions. Something that relaxes you to the maximum.

•Try doing something you wouldn't normally do, something which is completely unlike you; try out new activities or sports that you have been curious about but haven't give a shot to yet.

• An exercise routine is extremely important. This may be something as basic as going for a walk at the park or yoga.

• Set yourself goals to get ahead and whenever you manage to achieve them, remember to give yourself a small reward.

• Keep using positive affirmations during the day to instil self-confidence and positive ideas and feelings.

• Look to find the best in bad situations, even in difficult situations there is probably something new that you might be able to learn or discover.

• Keep in mind that the problem won't last forever, and it is just a temporary stage. Difficult situations seldom last for a long time.

Being limitless and committed

Remember that in many circumstances, the biggest difference between you and others that are able to accomplish great things, is that they haven't put the same mental barriers as you do and don't carry limiting beliefs that cripple their success. Be committed. You need to take positive action and choose just what it is you want to attain in existence and set your ultimate goal. Once you've done this, you need to get into it with utter conviction and commitment. When you plan and set your ultimate goal you need firm conviction that you'll achieve it, no matter whatever it takes. Try visualizing your goal from beginning to end and see yourself achieving whatever it is you're interested in.

Developing creativity

Although it may sound surprising to some, everybody has a creative side, although can be sometimes hidden or not as obvious as it is for others. Nevertheless, you can do a lot to spark creativeness by and practicing a few simple things. By developing your creativity, you will help keep the mind healthily entertained and it will have a positive carryover to whenever you're trying to reinforce optimistic thinking. Here are a few some tips that will help you expand and develop your creative side:

• Create lists - you are able to expand your creativeness greatly and get that side working by looking into making up a lists whenever you're facing a challenge or problem which needs a bit of creative thinking; write down as many ideas as you can think of for finding solutions to challenges.

• Embrace changes in your life- it's easy to get creative blocks when stuck inside a monotonous routine. Try to implement small changes in your life to get a different perspective on things.

• Work with groups – working in a group and brainstorming together is an excellent way to promote creative thinking.

• Positively challenge yourself and others – Instead of doing the same things over and over again. Ask yourself why you are doing them and challenge yourself to embrace taking a different approach. The same applies with the people that you interact with on your day to day life. If you feel like they can make an improvement by taking a different approach on things, try suggesting them some ideas and see where it takes you.

• Doodle - if you're having trouble finding solutions to a challenging event in your life, then have a paper and pen handy and allow set your imagination free by doodling thoughts and ideas. You'll be surprised at the things you may come up with after doing this activity.

• Life coaches - if you think your creativeness is really depleted, then you might consider consulting with a life coach for advice. Competent life coaches can easily help you by putting you on the right path again.

• What would a child do? - forget about all of your adult obligations, stresses, strains and worries and return to your childhood for a moment and ask yourself what would a small child do in that situation; children possess some of the most creative minds and their imaginations know no bounds.

• Relax – one of the biggest creativity killers is stress. Unfortunately, in our hectic world, stress is probably one of the most common occurrences. If necessary, go on a short vacation as it will help clear your thoughts, relax and give you a new perspective to life's challenges.

• Play games- some games such as logic puzzles can be an excellent way of taking your mind off a problem and boost creative thinking. Whenever you're solving a logic puzzle, your mind will have little time to worry about something else.

Creativeness Tips and Sources

Just about everybody can benefit from creativeness within their lives. You should be using creativity to assist with work projects, set goals, manage your personal life and a lot more. To help with this, here are a few tips to further enhance creativity in your life.

1. Remain Healthy - Find a physical activity that you enjoy and try to stick with it. Change it out when you wish to, but carry on doing some kind of exercise. Get enough rest. Eat a number of well balanced meals. Meditation or something similar you enjoy to do for mental relaxation will help a lot.

2. Be curious – Start asking yourself questions about things that are part of your normal day to day life. Why? How? What would happen if? Try to find

the answers to these questions and keep a journal to track all of your discoveries.

3. Read something new – When looking for a new book, choose something that you wouldn't usually read. For those who have always leaned towards nonfiction, try reading a fiction book. There are plenty of interesting books to see and a wide variety of genres to select from. If you have access to a library, your librarian will gladly assist you to explore new books. Online, there are plenty of forums with members that will help you with suggestions that you might not have thought of otherwise.

4. It's ok to behave like a child sometimes– We've talked about how thinking like a child can help you, but also behaving like one can be an excellent way to help you feel free and creative. Youngsters are seldom worried about things, are always honest and love to have fun. Consider the things you did as a child that brought you great joy. Start drawing or

painting, go to the amusement park or whatever that would have brought you a great deal of satisfaction!

5. Play 'what if?' –What if your last day on earth was tomorrow? Let's say you probably did visit college for business? If aliens where real? Constitute your personal 'what if?' questions and see where your mind goes.

6. Never Assume Anything. Assumptions can be a sure way of getting into trouble. You may think that your manager is really a jerk. What if he's having hard times in his personal life and that's the reason why he's taking it out on his employees? You may think that the one who cut you off in the morning was inconsiderate. What if he was taking his child to the doctor for an emergency?

7. Write about yourself – Just exactly who are
    you? What sort of person are you currently?
    What things have you gone though in life?
    Have you thought why you do things the way
    you currently do them? Writing down and
    answering all of these questions can help
    bring awareness and creativity into your life.

8. Really listen. Instead of waiting for your
    turn to speak, listen closely whenever your
    engaging in a conversation with others. Stop
    and think for a moment what must be this
    person's everyday life? Imagine the way they
    live and think.

Paying attention to your inner ideas

Everyone has feelings about stuff that take place in
their day to day lives. They could either be
discouraging ideas or they may be positive ones. An

easy example of this would be when you dress up for a special night out. Whenever you're trying out clothes for the occasion and see yourself in the mirror, you instantly think "wow, I look wonderful" or shake your head and select other clothes. This is one of the simplest forms of hearing your inner ideas or intuition with regards to picking what might be best for you.

However we are able to put our inner ideas to a lot of good uses within our day-to-day lives when we focus on tuning into them. Our inner ideas might help us to achieve great things in life, be more confident and live a more joyful, productive and fulfilling existence.

You're one of the best resources you have in life with regards to making the best choices and also the right choices. You are able to instantly determine if something's wrong or right by hearing your own intuition. Being in tune with your intuition is not that complicated, and here are a few simple methods for you to begin using it:

• One of the simplest ways to develop your intuition is to use it to make choices for less important decisions, examples might be, selecting what you would like for supper or which movie or restaurant to visit.

• It will be simpler to tune into yourself and your inner ideas when it's quiet, so select a room in which you know you will not be disturbed with regards to making important choices and decisions. A great technique is to close your eyes and take few deep breaths and then focus completely on the issue or task at hands and find out what are the first things that pop in your mind.

• Think about all the times you've thought 'I wish I had followed my gut feeling.' While it is true that intuition can be right most of the times, sometimes you will inevitably make the wrong choice by following it. Sometimes this happens because you might have misinterpreted your inner thoughts. Try to come up with the thoughts that might have been misinterpreted and learn from your mistakes.

• When letting your inner guidance come through don't confuse matters if you attempt way too hard or sway the answer one way or another. Odds are if you're heavily leaning towards one way, you already have the solution.

The more you are in tune and aware with your inner guidance, the easier it will be to make the right decision when you decide to use it. It is mostly whenever we start to lose belief and doubt ourselves that people we get stuck and indecisive, which usually leads to the wrong direction.

Mental imagery works

Probably one the most effective and inspirational tools that you can use daily is our personal imagination. Your personal ideas, insights, ideas and intuition may be used inside your daily existence to create positive changes for the better in almost any facet of your life. Everybody has an imagination and although some people possess a more vivid one which is activated faster than it does for others, after some practice, we all can use it to our benefit.

How to use imagination as a tool

The way you use imagination to your advantage in day to day life is only limited by yourself. You can and should use your imagination to visualize a different number of things and use it in several situations. For example, you can use visualization to form an optimistic picture of the result of any event so that you can feed your brain positive thoughts before actually going through that situation in real life. If done correctly, you can even replace any negative thoughts you had previously with it. You should practice visualization as much as you can and look at the imagery from several angles and perspectives. The imagery should be as clear and detailed as possible and show the outcome that you wish. Consider your imagination and the mental picture you build like a blueprint for developing and building on, just like a designer utilizes a blueprint when planning a project from beginning to end.

Foundations

Begin by thinking about the foundations of your idea/project or whatever it is that you wish to change and without rush, start by slowly building up from the bottom, clearly picturing every single detail of it. When doing so, ask these questions to yourself:

• What exactly is it just that I wish to achieve or change?

• What difference will this make in the end?

• Is it possible for me to achieve this on my own?

• What changes must I do in my life to accomplish this?

• Is there something I need to learn to accomplish this?

After you have laid the foundation for whatever it is that you want to change in your life, then go ahead and build up on it.

Important things about mental imagery

The most important thing to keep in mind whenever you want to use mental imagery successfully are:

• Focusing your imagination on a single idea at a time.

• Developing an extremely clear and detailed mental picture of the concept and outcome in your thoughts.

• Steadily building up on the idea from beginning to completion.

• Successfully executing what you visualized.

Chapter4: Controlling Fears and Phobias

Just about everyone has a strong fear/phobia or a few of them. Whether it is rodents, a visit to the dentist or public speaking, even the person that tries to act tough all the time probably has a fear somewhere. In the majority of cases, these fears are minor and are no cause of major concern whatsoever. However when fears become so severe they cause tremendous anxiety and hinder your quality of life, several problems may arise. These strong fears can sometimes develop into phobias. The good thing is that phobias and fears can be treated and managed most of the time. Certain self-help strategies and therapy will help you overcome your fears so that you can start enjoying life more.

What exactly are phobias?

Phobias are intense levels of fear attributed to certain things which in most cases pose little to no danger. Perhaps some of the most phobias and fears include being in tight spaces, bridges, highway driving, snakes, and visits to the dentist. However, can develop out of almost anything. Most phobias develop in early childhood, but they may also develop in grown-ups.

Those that suffer from phobias or intense fear of certain situations most likely understand that the fear is irrational, yet they aren't able to control their feelings. The simple act of visualizing the feared object or situation can make them feel uncontrollably anxious. This visualization sometimes goes on for a lot of time and repetition, and if there ever comes a moment when they are actually exposed to their fear in real life, the feeling of terror becomes very powerful and overwhelming.

Being exposed to the fear is so terrifying that they might go through great lengths in order to avoid these very uncomfortable situations. The downside is that people will greatly inconvenience themselves or perhaps alter their way of life negatively. For those who have claustrophobia, for instance, they may turn down a good job offer if there's a need to ride the elevator to get to work. For those who have feelings of anxiety with heights, they may drive an additional 20 miles to prevent a tall bridge.

Understanding your fear is the first and most important milestone to overcoming it. It's vital that you realize that phobias are fairly typical among people. (You're definitively not crazy if you have one) It may also help to understand that phobias are highly treatable. You are able to overcome nervousness and fear, regardless of how unmanageable it feels at the moment.

The differences between "normal" fears and phobias or "irrational" fears

It is perfectly normal as well as useful to us for fear to be called upon in your body whenever you're facing a dangerous situation. Fear is an adaptive response that has helped us a lot through evolution. It has a unique safety purpose - to activate the automated "fight-or-flight" response. Once our bodies feel this response, we are able to respond quickly to the challenging situation we're facing and thus, be better able to protect ourselves in case of a threat.

However, the issue with phobias is that the threat is greatly exaggerated or non-existent. For instance, it is common to become scared of a snarling Rottweiler, but it's irrational to become afraid of the friendly dog on the leash, as you may be for those who have your dog fear.

Normal fears in youngsters

Many childhood fears are natural and have a tendency to build up at specific ages. For instance, many small children fear so much the dark that they need a light source to be able to sleep. That does not mean that what they're experiencing is a phobia. Generally, they'll outgrow this fear as they age.

In case that your child's fear isn't disturbing their daily existence or causing him or her a lot of distress, then there's little reason to be very concerned about it. However, when the fear is disturbing your child's social activities, school performance, or sleep, you might want to visit a qualified child counselor.

Some common types of phobias and fears

Animal phobias

People are commonly afraid of mice, spiders, insects, but sometimes even house animals such as dogs or cats.

Environmental phobias

Some common examples are fear of heights, being in dark places, water, fire.

Situational

Claustrophobia is perhaps the most common example of a situational phobia, which is fear of enclosed spaces. Other common situational phobias are flying or driving on the highway.

Social phobias

Social phobias or social anxiety is a fear of being in social situations where you might be shamed or judged. For those who have social fear, they might be excessively self-conscious and scared of humiliating yourself before others. Nervousness over how to act and whatever others will think may make you avoid certain social situations you'd otherwise enjoy.

Anxiety about speaking in public is sometimes linked to social phobias. Other fears connected with social fear include anxiety about eating in public places, speaking to other people, taking exams, mingling in a party, and being asked something in a classroom or event.

Signs and signs and symptoms of phobias

The signs and symptoms of intense fear can vary from mild feelings of apprehension and anxiety to a full-blown feeling of terror where the sufferer is unable to do anything. Typically, the closer you're towards whatever it is you're scared of, the higher your levels of fear are going to be. Your fear may also be greater if there's no way to avoid the uncomfortable situation.

Seeking help to cure phobias and fears

Although phobias are typical, they usually won't considerably disrupt your existence. For instance, for those who have a fear of poisonous snakes, you can live a normal life if you reside in a town in which you will not encounter one. However, for those who have a serious fear of crowded areas, being forced to move to a large city would pose a severe issue.

In case your fear doesn't really impact your day to day living too much, it's most likely nothing to lose sleep over. But when avoiding the situation, event or thing that creates your fear disrupts your quality of life, or keeps you against doing stuff you would like to, it's probably time for you to look for a solution.

Consider taking action into finding help to cure your phobia/fear if:

It causes intense and disabling fear, anxiety, and panic

You already know that the fear is excessive and not reasonable

You avoid specific situations and places from your fear

Your avoidance disrupts your normal routine or causes significant distress

You've had the fear not less than six several weeks

Self-help or therapy for phobias: which to choose?

With regards to treating phobias, self-help strategies and therapy can both work. What's good for you depends upon numerous factors, including the seriousness of your fear, your insurance policy, and the total support needed.

Typically, self-assistance is usually worth a shot. The greater the amount of things you can do on your own, the greater you'll feel in control of your life, which is excellent when dealing with phobias and also for reducing negative thinking. However, in the case your fear is really severe and it triggers anxiety attacks or unmanageable anxiety, you might want to get external help

The good thing is that therapy for phobias includes has a great deal of success, whether it is done by yourself or a professional. Not only that, but you'll be able to see results very quickly, sometimes within the first 2-5 sessions.

However, support isn't found exclusively within in the form of a professional counselor. Having a trusted family member or a friend by your side helping you can be amazingly helpful.

Fear self-help tip 1: Face your fears by taking tiny steps at a time.

Of course you'll want to do whatever it takes to avoid the situation you fear. But regarding conquering phobias, the cliché is actually true: facing your fears is paramount. While avoidance may cause you to feel better within the short-term, it prevents you against realizing that the fear might not be as frightening or overwhelming as you originally thought it would be. You won't develop your ability to cope with your fears and take control of your life by constantly avoiding them. Consequently, the fear never stops growing in your mind, and whenever the time comes where you are forced to face it, the situation will be much worse.

The best way to beat a fear is as simple as progressively and frequently exposing you to whatever it is you're afraid of in a controlled and safe environment. In this exposure process, you'll learn how to ride the anxiety waves until the uncomfortable event passes.

Through repeated encounters facing your fear, you'll start to understand that the worst isn't going to take place or in other words, that you aren't going to die or lose whatever it is you're afraid of. With every exposure, you'll start feeling more and more in control and confident when facing the situation. After a few encounters, the fear will lose its power dramatically.

Effectively facing your fears takes planning, practice, and persistence.

How to climb the fear/phobia ladder.

If you've attempted exposure previously and you weren't successful, you might have begun with something too frightening or overwhelming. It's important to start with a scenario that you could handle, and start to slowly climb the ladder as you build your confidence and coping skills while you progress.

Create a list. Create a list from the frightening situations associated with your fear. If you are scared of flying, your list may include things associated to the event, such as booking your ticket, packing your suitcase, driving towards the airport terminal, watching the planes, dealing with security, boarding the plane, and hearing the flight attendant present the security instructions.

How to construct your fear ladder. Arrange the things in your list from least frightening to most terrifying. The initial thing should cause you slight feelings of discomfort or anxiety, but you shouldn't be so frightened that you're too intimidated to put it to test. When designing the ladder, it may be useful to consider your end goal (for instance, to be able to fly without panicking) and then all the small steps necessary to be able to get there.

How to work your way up. Begin with step #1 (within this example, searching videos of people getting inside planes and then videos of planes taking off) and don't move to the next unless you're feeling more comfortable. The more you confront your fear on the step you're currently at, the easier it will be to move to the next step. Probably in little time you'll notice that you'll start getting used to it and the feelings of anxiety and nervousness will start to vanish. If you're dealing with a fear that has a short duration (for instance, crossing bridges), get it done again and again until the discomfort starts vanishing. Using the bridge example, the first step could be watching videos of people crossing bridges; the next step would be for you to cross a very, very small bridge. Once you've done a certain step on several separate occasions without feeling an excessive amount of anxiety, you'll be able to proceed to the next phase. If you're finding your steps to be too difficult, always remember that you can break them down into lower and smaller sized steps or proceed at a much slower pace.

Practice. It's vital that you practice regularly. The greater the frequency of your practice, the faster you'll be able to move to the next step of the ladder. However, there's no need to excessively rush things. Go in a pace that you are able to manage without feeling overwhelmed or emotionally drained after each session.

And don't forget: you'll feel uncomfortable and anxious while you face your fears; however the feelings are just temporary. If you keep at it, the anxiety will eventually fade. Your fears will start having little to no effect on you.

Let's take a look at an example of a 'fear ladder' using arachnophobia (fear of spiders). We'll try to use as many steps as possible, since this can be a very tough phobia to overcome.

Step One: Take a look at drawings of spiders.

Step Two: See real life pictures of spiders. The pictures shouldn't be zoomed in and detailed.

Step Three: Look at zoomed in and detailed pictures of spiders.

Step Four: Watch videos of spiders in their natural habitats.

Step Five: Watch pictures of spiders in normal households.

Step Six: Stand 6 ft from a spider at a pet shop or wherever you can find spiders securely inside a cage.

Step Seven: Similar to the previous step, but this time stand 3 ft from it.

Step Eight: Get close to the spider and observe it.

Step Nine: Watch someone handle a harmless pet spider from 3 ft away from it.

Step Ten: Get close to the person and the spider.

Step Eleven: At this point, your fear of spiders will be greatly diminished and you may even choose to touch one, and thus reducing your fear even further.

Should you begin to feel overwhelmed...

While it's natural to feel scared or anxious while you face your fear, if you're finding that you're getting emotionally drained after a session immediately back away and employ the strategy outlined below to rapidly calm your central nervous system.

Fear Self-help tip: Learn how to relax quickly

When you are feeling afraid or anxious, you'll have a number of uncomfortable physical signs and symptoms, like a racing heart and a suffocating feeling in more extreme cases. These physical sensations could be frightening themselves-and are a large part of why fears and phobias can wreak havoc inside our lives. However, by finding out how to relax quickly, you will be able to be more confident on your capabilities for tolerating uncomfortable sensations when facing your fears.

An easy breathing exercise

When you are anxious, you have a tendency to take quick, shallow breaths (which is also referred to as hyperventilating). This can dramatically increase the physical feelings of tension. By breathing deeply in the abdomen, you are able to reverse these undesirable sensations. You can actually start practicing this relaxation technique without needing to feel nervous or anxious. In fact, it can be an excellent idea to practice and be familiar with it before you apply it to a real life situation. After just a couple of short minutes of breathing using this method, you'll feel less tense and anxious. This technique can also be used whenever you're feeling overwhelmed by stress or negative thoughts.

Here's how to do it:

1. Start by either sitting or standing with your back straight. Place a hand near the chest area and the other one over your stomach.

2. Count to four and take a very slow breath through the nose, not the mouth. The hand placed over your stomach should rise. On the other hand, the hand over the chest should hardly move.

3. Hold your breath for 6-8 seconds.

4. Exhale using your mouth and count for 7-9 seconds, pushing out all the air you can while contracting your stomach muscles. The hands in your stomach should be moving while you exhale, however your other hand should hardly move.

5. Inhale again, and repeat the cycle until you start feeling more calm and relaxed.

Practice this breathing exercise for 4-6 minutes at least two times per day. Once you're confident with the technique, you can begin applying it whenever you are facing a fear or other uncomfortable situations.

Make use of your senses

Among the quickest and most efficient methods to relieve anxiety can be to simply engage a number of your senses -sight, seem, taste, smell, touch, or movement. Since everybody has a different body, it's important to perform some experimenting to find out what works well with you.

Movement - Take a stroll, do some jumping, or light stretching. Focusing while doing other physical activities such as dancing, drumming, and running could be especially good at relieving anxiety.

Sight - Take a look at something that relaxes you or enables you to smile: a nice landscape, family photos, cute pictures or videos of animals on the web.

Listen - Pay attention to soothing music, sing a popular tune, or play an instrument. Or you may also focus on the relaxing sounds of nature (either live or recorded): sea waves, wind going through leaves, wild birds singing.

Smell - Light scented candle lights. Smell the flowers inside a garden. When outdoors, try inhaling the outdoors.

Taste – Indulge in your favourite snack, savoring each bite. Slowly drink a warm mug of coffee or teas. Chew on your favourite bubble gum. Have a mint or perhaps your favourite dessert.

Touch - Have a hands or neck massage. Cuddle with your partner. Wrap yourself inside a soft blanket. Sit outdoors and feel the breeze.

Meditation for anxiety and stress relief

Meditation has been used for many reasons, one of the primary ones being as a relaxation technique that will help decrease anxiety. It has a multitude of other benefits such as improving your energy, mood and focus. With regular practice, meditation will help boost parts of the mind that are responsible for feeling more calm, assisting to quell fear and panic before they strike.

Fear self-help tip: Challenge negative ideas

Understanding how to challenge negative thoughts is a vital part of overcoming your fear. If you have a fear or a phobia, you'll have a tendency to overestimate how bad the real situation will be if you're ever exposed to it. Simultaneously, you underestimate your abilities in coping with difficult situations.

Ideas that trigger and fuel phobias are often negative and rarely are they actually realistic. It can be helpful to test out these thoughts. Start by writing lower any negative ideas you get when faced together with your fear. You'll find that these ideas tend to fall under these categories:

Fortune telling. For instance, "This Bridge will collapse" "I'll embarrass myself in front of others" "I will certainly lose it once I'm inside the elevator and the doors are shut."

Overgeneralization. "I fainted once whilst getting my blood drawn" "I'll never be able to go through blood tests without passing out" "That dog just lunged at me. Most dogs are probably going to bite me."

Catastrophizing. "The captain stated we're dealing with turbulence. The plane will crash!" "The man alongside me coughed. Maybe he has something contagious. I will end up sick!"

Once you've identified your negative ideas, evaluate them. Make use of the following examples to begin.

Negative thought: "The elevator will break lower and I'll get trapped and suffocate."

Can I think about any hard evidence that contradicts this negative thought?

"I see lots of people go through their day to day lives by using elevators and they have never broken down."

"I can't think about anybody dying from suffocation while inside an elevator."

"I haven't really experienced being in an elevator that has had a severe malfunction."

"There are air vents within an elevator that will promote air flow."

Would you do anything whatsoever to solve this case whether it does occur?

"I could probably press the alarm button or make use of the telephone to call for help."

Are you currently creating a false belief?

"Yes. I'm incorrectly fortune telling, since I don't have any evidence whatsoever that the elevator will break or malfunction."

If you have a friend that has this fear, what would you tell him?

"I would most likely state that the likelihood of it happening is extremely slim as you rarely hear about people being trapped in elevators."

It is also useful to generate some positive thoughts to cope with the situation that you could tell yourself when facing your fear. For instance:

"I've felt this way several times before and absolutely nothing terrible happened. It might be uncomfortable, but it won't cause any harm to me."

"If the worst happens and I get a panic attack while I'm driving, I'll simply pull over and wait for the discomfort to pass."

"I've traveled in several occasions and the plane has never crashed. Actually, I do not know anybody that has you been inside a plane crash. Statistically, flying is extremely safe."

Conclusion

I hope that you have found it useful on your journey to find yourself in a better state of mental and emotional health.

Please remember that if you have made consistent efforts to enhance your emotional and mental health by following the advice in this book or other sources and you are still not functioning optimally in your family life, work, and your relationships, then it might be time for you to seek specialist help. Even if you do, strongly consider continuing to practice the methods talked about in this book. In some instances where there's a definite lack of motivation, seeking the help of a professional can be the only way to get going.